Paddington's
Things I Feel
by Michael Bond

Illustrated by John Lobban

 HarperFestival
A Division of HarperCollins*Publishers*

PADDINGTON'S THINGS I FEEL
Text copyright © 1994 by Michael Bond
Illustrations copyright © 1994 by HarperCollins Publishers Ltd.
First published in Great Britain by HarperCollins Publishers Ltd. in 1994
Printed and bound in Hong Kong.
All rights reserved.
First American edition, 1994

I feel excited

I feel hungry

I feel scared

I feel happy

I feel worried

I feel brave

I feel upset

25¢
a throw

I feel dizzy

I feel strong

I feel jammed

I feel surprised

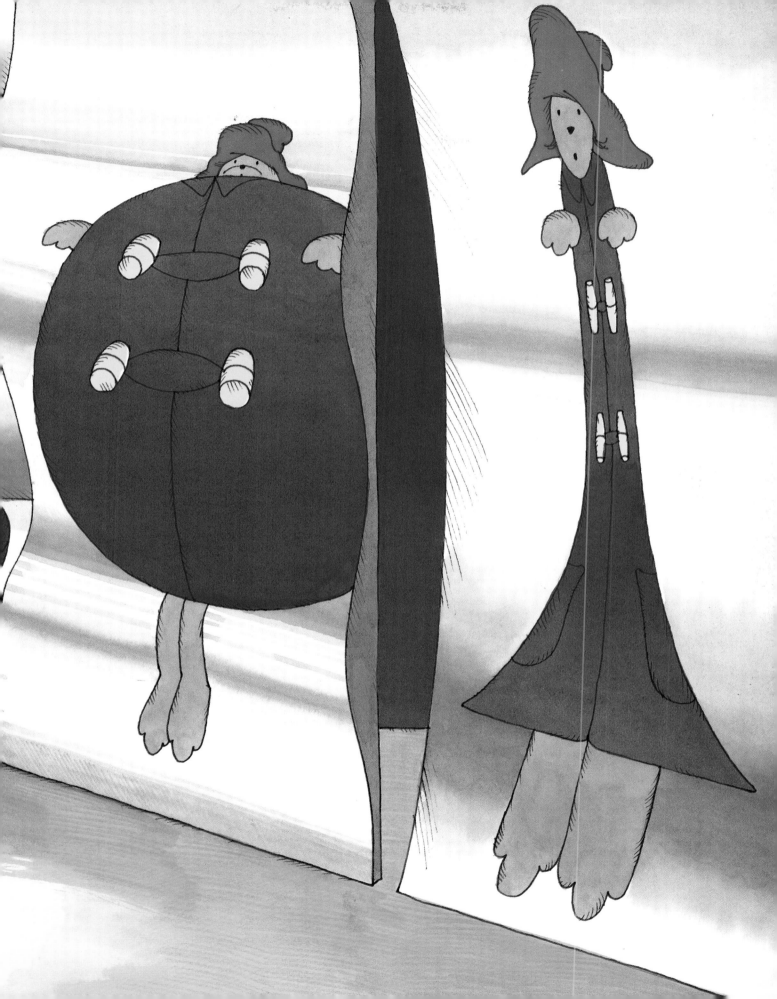

I feel dreamy

I feel lost

I feel safe

I feel sad

I feel sleepy